NUMBER, NUMBER, CUT A CUCUMBER

by

Nick Toczek

CABOODLE BOOKS LTD

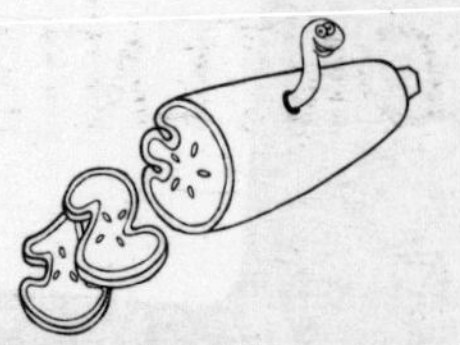

First published in Great Britain in 2009
by Caboodle Books Ltd

A Catalogue record for this book is available from the British Library.

ISBN 978-0-9562656-4-7

Illustrations and front cover by Al Jacques
Page Layout by Highlight Type Bureau Ltd
Printed by CPI Group (UK) Ltd, Croydon, CR0 4YY

The paper and board used in the paperback by Caboodle Books Ltd are natural recyclable products made from wood grown in sustainable forests. The manufacturing processes conform to the environmental regulations of the country of origin.

Caboodle Books Ltd
Riversdale, 8 Rivock Avenue, Steeton, BD20 6SA
www.authorsabroad.com

CONTENTS

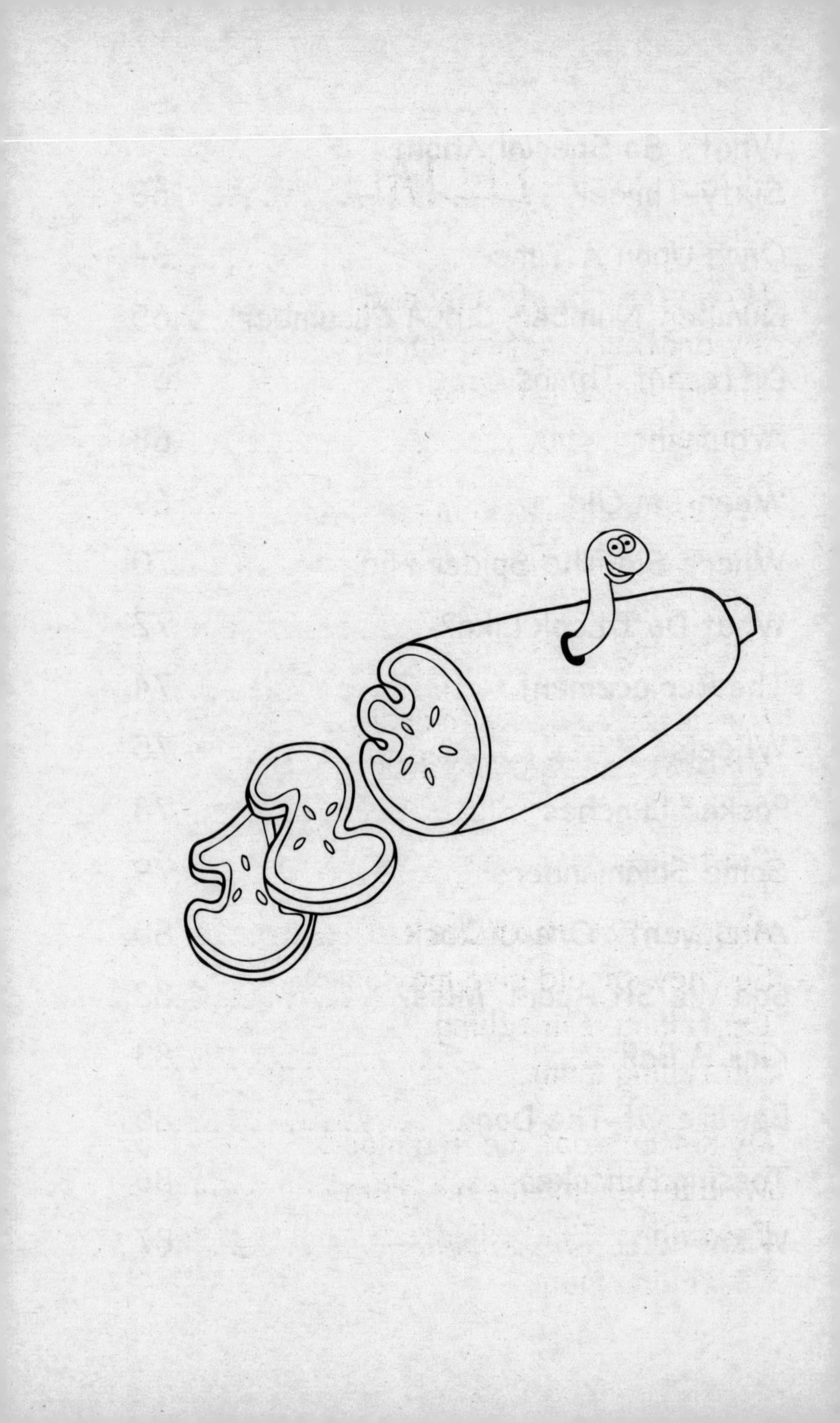

TELLTALE

My sister's being silly and
My brother's acting dumb.
I'm telling. I'm telling.
I'm telling mum.

And the biscuit tin is empty.
There's not a single crumb.
I'm telling. I'm telling.
I'm telling mum.

My sister took my tricycle.
My brother's got my drum.
I'm telling. I'm telling.
I'm telling mum.

And both of them are eating sweets
So they should give me some.
I'm telling. I'm telling.
I'm telling mum.

My sister's got me in a mood.
My brother makes me glum.
I'm telling. I'm telling.
I'm telling mum.

They always get the things they want.
Now they've got chewing gum.
I'm telling. I'm telling.
I'm telling mum.

My sister slammed the door on me.
She nearly trapped my thumb.
I'm telling. I'm telling.
I'm telling mum.

My brother's taken off his shoes
And his socks really hum.
I'm telling. I'm telling.
I'm telling mum.

My sister's eating apples now.
My brother's got a plum.
I'm telling. I'm telling.
I'm telling mum.

Cos they won't give me any fruit
And I've an empty tum.
I'm telling. I'm telling.
I'm telling mum.

I CAN COUNT

I can count to one
With a currant bun. *(put imaginary bun in mouth and loudly munch)*

I can count to two
With me and you. *(point to self, then someone else)*

I can count to three.
Bumble-bee. *(flap hands at shoulder-level, like wings)*

I can count to four.
Give a loud ROAR. *(pronounce ROAR as a long, loud growl)*

I can count to five.
Watch me drive. *(hands to mime turning a steering-wheel)*

I can count to six.
Juggling tricks. *(hands to mime juggling with balls or clubs)*

I can count to seven.
Point to Heaven. *(pointing upwards)*

I can count to eight.
Concentrate. *(hunched up, with one fist against forehead)*

I can count to nine.
Do the happy sign. *(thumbs up)*

I can count to ten. *(holding up all ten fingers and thumbs)*
Let's do that again...

I can count to one
With a currant bun. *(put imaginary bun in mouth and loudly munch)*

I can count to two
With me and you. *(point to self, then someone else)*

I can count to three.
Bumble-bee. *(flap hands at shoulder-level, like wings)*

I can count to four.
Give a loud ROAR. *(pronounce ROAR as a long, loud growl)*

I can count to five.
Watch me drive. *(hands to mime turning a steering-wheel)*

I can count to six.
Juggling tricks. *(hands to mime juggling with balls or clubs)*

I can count to seven.
Point to Heaven. *(pointing upwards)*

I can count to eight.
Concentrate. *(hunched up, with one fist against forehead)*

I can count to nine.
Do the happy sign. *(thumbs up)*

I can count to ten. *(holding up all ten fingers and thumbs)*
Thank you, ladies and gentlemen.
(bowing slowly and grandly)

IT'S FREEZING COLD

It's far too cold to get out of bed.
My toes'll be frozen. My nose'll be red.

I'll stay snuggled up all day instead.
You'll never see more than the top of my head.

I'll be quite alright so long as I'm fed.
So bring me a drink and a slice of bread.

But I bet you the butter
won't even spread.
And my milk'll be more like a lump of lead.

It's far too cold to get out of bed.
My toes'll be frozen. My nose'll be red.

So leave me alone. You heard what I said.
I'm under the covers and cuddling ted.

Did someone say 'snowing'?
I'm out of bed.
Got boots on, gloves on,
sledge from the shed.

I'm not going to lie there like I'm dead.
I'm spending the day outside instead.

My toes'll be frozen. My nose'll be red.
But it's far too nice for staying in bed.

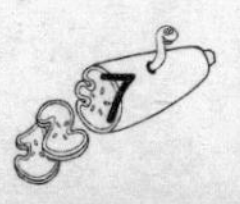

NOTICING NOISES

Flip-flops flap
Slip-slap-slop.
Taps go *drip-drap*
Drop by drop.

Planes go *knee-ow-mmmm!*
Sleepers snore.
Firemen's sirens
Go nee-naw!

Pianos plink
Plunk-plank-plonk.
Cars and geese go
Honk! Honk! Honk!

Ghosts go *woooh!*
Soup spoons slurp.
Fizzy drinks'll
Make us burp.

Cows go *moo.*
Pigs go *oink.*
Kangaroos go
Boink! Boink! Boink!

Front doors slam.
Church bells ring.
Thrushes, choirs and
Pop stars sing.

Babies bawl.
Barn owls hoot.
Cheap tin whistles
Go *Toot! Toot!*

Toilets flush.
Puddles splash.
Drumsticks bash *Bash!*
Bash! Bash! Bash!

Teachers talk,
Talk and talk.
Pirates' parrots
Speak and squawk.

People shout.
Sheep'll baa.
Laugh at them. *Go*
Ha! Ha! Ha!

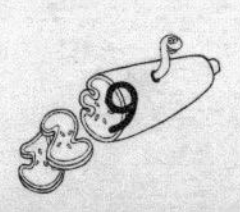

SENT TO BED

Sadly sitting on a stair.
Sadly with my teddy bear.
Sadly cos it isn't fair.
We're up here and they're down there.

NOBODY HERE

Where's Jed? Still in bed.
Where's John? Come and gone.
Where's Jean? Not been seen.
Where's Jan? In Japan.
Where's Joan? On the phone.
Where's Jack? Won't be back.

Where's Jake? On his break.
Where's Jill? Absent still.
Where's Jude? Fetching food.
Where's Joy? Out with Roy.
Where's Jim? Cops took him.
Where's Jay? Went away.

Where's James? Playing games.
Where's Jess? Changed address.
Where's Jock? Died of shock.
Where's Jane? Can't explain.
Where's Jules? Broke the rules.
Where's Jill? Absent still.

Where's Jade? Been delayed.
Where's June? Honeymoon.
Where's Jen? Gone again.
Where's Judd? Caked in mud.
Where's Jem? Bethlehem.
Where's Josh? Somewhere posh.

Where's Joe? Had to go.
Where's Jeff? Oh-eff-eff.
Where's Jazz? Meeting Baz.
Where's Joss? With the boss.
Where's Jez? Sick, he says.
Where's Jeb? On The Web.

Where are you? On the loo.

THE BIG PARADE

In the big parade there were:
Seventy-six trombones and xylophones,
Seventy-six children with ice-cream cones,
Seventy-six aunt Janes and Jeans and Joans,
Seventy-six men using mobile phones,
Seventy-six Lion Kings on Lion King thrones,
Seventy-six pop stars with microphones,
Seventy-six speedboats with engine drones,
Seventy-six pale ghosts and their
  gravestones,
Seventy-six Playstation levels and zones,
Seventy-six punk bands called The
  Undertones,
Seventy-six pirate ships flying
  skull'n'crossbones,
Seventy-six Harry Potters with
  philosopher's stones,
And seventy-six children giving loud
  groans
Packed off to bed amid moody moans.

SULKING

Oh, leave me alone cos I don't want to
play.
I'm sat on my own and I've nothing to say.
I'm nobody's friend for the rest of today.
So just put my tea over there on a tray.
And tell the whole world that I said: "Go
away!"

THE CHILD WHO PRETENDED TO BE A DRAGON

My mum and dad got angry
And they told me not to lie,
When I said that I'd grown wings
And was learning how to fly.

They said I should be sensible
And stop making a fuss,
After I'd announced that I was green
And longer than a bus.

And they turned around and told me
I was not to tell tall tales,
When they heard that I'd been claiming
That my skin was growing scales.

Then both of them got cross with me
And each called me a liar,
Just because I mentioned
I'd been breathing smoke and fire.

But they finally got flaming mad,
They really hit the roof
When I rushed at them with sharpened claws
And all my teeth, as proof.

My mum let out a piercing scream.
My dad began to rave.
So I ate them both. They tasted nice.
Then I flew off to live in a cave.

HOW DID I GET IN HERE?

(written with children from St Edmund's Nursery School, Bradford)

Did I climb in through the window?
Did I dig up through the floor?
Did I drop through a hole in the roof?
No! I walked in through the door.

WHAT GRANDADS ARE LIKE

Grandads grump and grumble.

They like apple crumble.
Their big bellies rumble.
They burp, belch and bumble.

They are rude, not humble.
They've rooms full of jumble:
Piles of junk that tumble.

And they fuss and fumble,
Shuffle round and stumble,
Mess about and mumble.

Grandpa-ly and grumpily,
Grandads grump and grumble.

WHEN THE SUN SHINES BLUE

On Mondays
When the sun shines blue
Crocodiles call out:
"Cock-a-doodle-do!"
Crocodiles call out:
"Cock-a-doodle-do!"

On Tuesdays
When the sun shines blue
Traffic lights try to
Kiss a kangaroo.
Traffic lights try to
Kiss a kangaroo.

On Wednesdays
When the sun shines blue
Water taps weep
"Waah-woo! Boo-hoo!"
Water taps weep
"Waah-woo! Boo-hoo!"

On Thursdays
When the sun shines blue
Thermometers sneeze:
"Achoo! Achoo!"
Thermometers sneeze:
"Achoo! Achoo!"

On Fridays
When the sun shines blue
Saucepans say:
"Oink! Baa! Woof! Moo!"
Saucepans say:
"Oink! Baa! Woof! Moo!"

On Saturdays
When the sun shines blue
Sweet shops sing:
"Stick a sock in my shoe!"
Sweet shops sing:
"Stick a sock in my shoe!"

On Sundays
When the sun shines blue
Swings in the park shout:
"Shut up, all of you!"
Swings in the park shout:
"Shut up, all of you!"

"Cock-a-doodle-do!"
"Cock-a-doodle-do!"
Kiss a kangaroo.
Kiss a kangaroo.
"Waah-woo! Boo-hoo!"
"Waah-woo! Boo-hoo!"
"Achoo! Achoo!"
"Achoo! Achoo!"
"Oink! Baa! Woof! Moo!"
"Oink! Baa! Woof! Moo!"
"Stick a sock in my shoe!"
"Stick a sock in my shoe!"
"Shut up, all of you!"
"Shut up, all of you!"

JUST BLAME DAD

When you're sleepy, weepy, sad,
Feeling moody, far from glad,
Don't get mad,
Just blame dad.

Worst weekend you've ever had,
Kept indoors cos weather's bad?
Don't get mad,
Just blame dad.

Sums for homework which won't add?
Someone scribbled on your pad?
Don't get mad,
Just blame dad.

Argued with some lass or lad?
Want what's in that TV ad?
Don't get mad,
Just blame dad.

THE SEVENTY-EIGHT BUS

"Driver! Driver! Do slow down!"
But he just wears an anxious frown
Cos he believes I'm running late.
And I'm the number seventy-eight,
Packed with passengers bound for town:
"Driver! Driver! Do slow down!"

And even when it snows and rains
I rattle along the country lanes.
Now watch the way I swerve and lurch
To take the curve around the church.

"Driver! Driver! Do slow down!"
But he just wears an anxious frown
Cos he believes I'm running late.
And I'm the number seventy-eight,
Packed with passengers bound for town:
"Driver! Driver! Do slow down!"

I come careering down the hill
And over the bridge beside the mill
And screeching round the roundabout
So people panic, shouting out:

"Driver! Driver! Do slow down!"
But he just wears an anxious frown
Cos he believes I'm running late.
And I'm the number seventy-eight,
Packed with passengers bound for town:
"Driver! Driver! Do slow down!"

FIRST DAY

Mum! Mum! Don't take me to school!
What if I'm punished for breaking a rule?
What if I fall off a chair or a stool?
What if the teachers are mad, mean and cruel?
What if I'm silly and act like a fool?
What if in swimming I'm pushed in the pool?

Wow! They're playing football, mum!
Isn't school cool!

POSH RESTAURANT

We're all agreed
We need to feed
And here's a place to try.
Oh, number, number,
Cut a cucumber
Riddly-diddly dye.

A table, please!
Bring bread'n'cheese,
And pass the parsnip pie.
Oh, number, number,
Cut a cucumber
Riddly-diddly dye.

My pricy slice
With spicy rice
Is nice, I can't deny.
Oh, number, number,
Cut a cucumber
Riddly-diddly dye.

They've brought the bill.
We all look ill.
The total's terribly high.
Oh, number, number,
Cut a cucumber
Riddly-diddly dye.

The whole amount's
Too much to count.
I think I'm going to cry.
Oh, number, number,
Cut a cucumber.
Riddly-diddly die.

ALL IN A LINE

Out for a stroll in the noonday sun
All alone, so that made one.

Then hop, hop, hop came a kangaroo.
Him plus me... well, we made two.

Then round our heads buzzed a bumble
bee.
Walk and hop and fly made three.

Then STOMP-STOMP-STOMP came a
dinosaur.
That's one more... not three but four.

Then another bee flew from the hive.
Buzz, buzz, buzz, buzz, buzz made five.

Then a magic man with tons of tricks
Tagged along and he made six.

Then an angel sent from Heaven
Joined our gang so we were seven.

Someone's mum in a *dreadful* state
Then turned up late which made us eight.

When we were chased by a porcupine
In a line from one to nine

We ran round the world and home, but
  then:
"Where've you been? It's half past ten!"

THE DRAGON WHO ATE OUR SCHOOL

The day the dragon came to call,
She ate the gate, the playground wall
And, slate by slate, the roof and all,
The staff room, gym, and entrance hall,
And every classroom, big or small.

So...
She's undeniably great,
She's absolutely cool,
The dragon who ate
The dragon who ate
The dragon who ate our school.

Pupils panicked. Teachers ran.
She flew at them with wide wingspan.
She slew a few and then began
To chew through the lollipop man,
Two parked cars and a transit van.

Wow... !
She's undeniably great,
She's absolutely cool,
The dragon who ate
The dragon who ate
The dragon who ate our school.

She bit off the head of the head.
She said she was sad he was dead.
He bled and he bled and he bled
And, as she fed, her chin went red
And then she swallowed the cycle shed.

Oh...
She's undeniably great,
She's absolutely cool,
The dragon who ate
The dragon who ate
The dragon who ate our school.

It's thanks to her that we've been freed.
We needn't write. We needn't read.
Me and my mates are all agreed,
We're very pleased with her indeed.
So, clear the way, let her proceed.

Cos...
She's undeniably great,
She's absolutely cool,
The dragon who ate
The dragon who ate
The dragon who ate our school.

There was some stuff she couldn't eat.
A monster forced to face defeat,
She spat it out along the street –
The dinner ladies' veg and meat
And that pink stuff they serve as sweet.

But...
She's undeniably great,
She's absolutely cool,
The dragon who ate
The dragon who ate
The dragon who ate our school.

SAYING SORRY

Once there was a little lad.
He'd be moody. He'd be bad.
He'd be rude to mum and dad,
Shout and scream and get so mad.

Then he'd see that they were sad
From the tantrum that he'd had,
So he'd hug them, then he'd add
"Sorry!" and they'd all be glad.

FOLDEROL

On the first
We cursed the ball
That burst against the garden wall.

On the second
We reckoned a small
Finger beckoned to one and all.

On the third
We heard the call
To sing the words to folderol.

On the fourth
We left Porthcawl
Heading north to Heptonstall.

Once rehearsed, now reversed:
Fourth to third to second to first...

On the fourth
We left Porthcawl
Heading north to Heptonstall.

On the third
We heard the call
To sing the words to folderol.

On the second
We reckoned a small
Finger beckoned to one and all.

On the first
We cursed the ball
That burst against the garden wall.

SOMETHING SCARY

Airy dairy telephonary.
Take a trip to Tipperary.
Tell me something slightly scary.
Might be nasty, naughty, sweary.
Ghastly witch with ghostly fairy.
Warty noses. Nostrils flary.
I don't cary, cary, cary.
I don't care a pink canary.

Airy dairy telephonary.
Take a trip to Tipperary.
Tell me something slightly scary.
Beastly, growly, grim and hairy.
Teeth and claws, and eyes all glary.
Something sort of grizzly-beary.
I don't cary, cary, cary.
I don't care a pink canary.

Airy dairy telephonary.
Take a trip to Tipperary.
Tell me something slightly scary.
Could be stories quite nightmary.
Creepy creatures, strange and stary.
I can bear it. I'm contrary.
I don't cary, cary, cary.
I don't care a pink canary.

GETTING OLD

While you're one
You're not much fun. *(shaking head)*
When you're two
You might just do. *(rocking outstretched hand, palm down)*

My friend Gillian
She's a silly 'un.
She told teacher
She was a million.

While you're one
You're not much fun. *(shaking head)*
When you're two
You might just do. *(rocking outstretched hand, palm down)*

If you're three
You're fine by me. *(thumbs up)*
Get to four
And I like you more. *(move facing palms apart)*

My dad's naughty
Calls me 'shorty'.
He's very old.
He's nearly forty.

While you're one
You're not much fun. *(shaking head)*
When you're two
You might just do. *(rocking outstretched hand, palm down)*

If you're three
You're fine by me. *(thumbs up)*
Get to four
And I like you more. *(move facing palms apart)*

Gimme five
To come alive. *(slap left palm with right palm)*

Six years old
Good as gold. *(pat top of head with right palm)*

When I get to be
About thirty-three
Gonna stay up all night
And watch TV.

While you're one
You're not much fun. *(shaking head)*
When you're two
You might just do. *(rocking outstretched hand, palm down)*

If you're three
You're fine by me. *(thumbs up)*
Get to four
And I like you more. *(move facing palms apart)*

Gimme five
To come alive. *(slap left palm with right palm)*

Six years old
Good as gold. *(pat top of head with right palm)*

Touching seven
Is total heaven.
After that...
You get old and fat!

BACK SOON

We've gone away
Till yesterday
But may be back before,
And when we call
We won't at all.
There's no one at the door.

Don't write because
Where we once was
We won't be any more.
The cards we sent
From where we went
All said: "So long, Senor."

So phone last week
When we shall speak
Of what we never saw.
We'll stand and stare
But won't be there.
So long to you, for sure.

CRUSHER

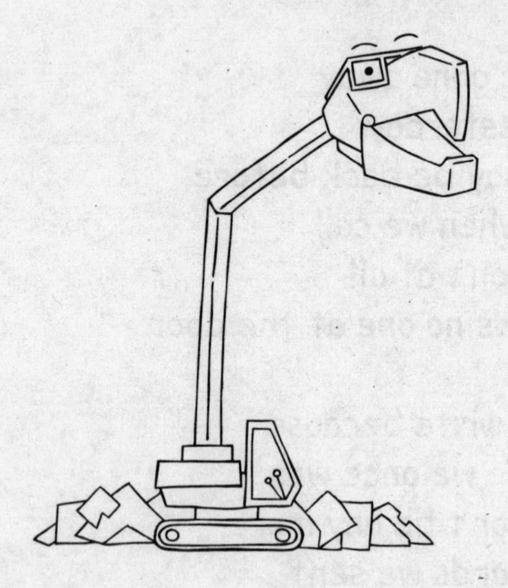

I'm a
huge hy-
draulic
crusher.

Read my
base I'm
made in
Russia.

Oiled out
of a
Texas
gusher.

Piston
puller.
Piston
pusher.

Function
like a
toilet
flusher.

I'm a
huge hy-
draulic
crusher.

Made to
be a
metal
musher.

My sur-
roundings
could be
plusher.

Scrap-yard
mud that
should be
lusher.

I work
slowly.
I'm no
rusher.

I'm a
huge hy-
draulic
crusher.

THE FOOTBALL FAMILY MAN

I'm the finest fan
That football's had.
I've a football gran
With a football fad.
I've a football mother
And a football dad,
And my football brother
Has football bad.

With my football wife
In our football pad,
To our football life
We football add
Two football daughters
And a football lad,
All football supporters,
All football mad.

We've football dogs.
They're football clad
In football togs
Like a football ad.
For our football ways,
We're football glad.
Without football days,
We'd be football sad.

I'm a football man
Who's football mad.
I'm the finest fan
That football's had.
I'm the football family man.

LOOKING FOR SIXTY-TWO

Has anyone here seen sixty-two?
Where can he be? I wish I knew.
We planned to meet outside the zoo
But he never turned up at our rendezvous
And now he's hours overdue.

Has anyone here seen sixty-two,
The house from Seventh Avenue?
His roof is red. His door is blue.
His garden's there, and the barbecue,
But the building's gone. It's strange but true.

Has anyone here seen sixty-two?
We've asked the others. We're asking you.
It's causing quite a hullabaloo.
The cops would like to interview
Whoever may have the slightest clue.

Has anyone here seen sixty-two?
He's disappeared like mountain dew,
Evaporated into the blue.
When he gets back, here's what we'll do.
We'll stick him in place with super-glue.

HOW THE BUMBLE BEE GOT HIS STRIPES

On the day that the world began,
Each of the creatures was shown
Every colour in the universe;
And all were told to choose
Which of these they wanted for
themselves.

Well, that day the elephant
Thought carefully and chose to be grey,
But the bumble bee
Just bumbled around and buzzed around
And couldn't make up his mind,
And the yellow sun shone so brightly
That the bumble bee's bum became yellow.

And that night the goldfish
Thought carefully and chose to be golden,
But the bumble bee
Just bumbled around and buzzed around
And couldn't make up his mind,
And the black night grew so dark
That the bumble bee's hips became black.

And next day the cricket
Thought carefully and chose to be green,
But the bumble bee
Just bumbled around and buzzed around
And couldn't make up his mind,
And the yellow sun shone so brightly
That the bumble bee's waist became
yellow.

And that night the owl
Thought carefully and chose to be brown,
But the bumble bee
Just bumbled around and buzzed around
And couldn't make up his mind,
And the black night grew so dark
That the bumble bee's chest became black.

And next day the polar bear
Thought carefully and chose to be white,
But the bumble bee
Just bumbled around and buzzed around
And couldn't make up his mind,
And the yellow sun shone so brightly
That the bumble bee's shoulders became yellow.

And that night the jay
Thought carefully and chose to be blue,
But the bumble bee
Just bumbled around and buzzed around
And couldn't make up his mind,
And the black night grew so dark
That the bumble bee's neck and head and legs became black.

And next day the bumble bee
Began to be thoughtful.
He bumbled around and buzzed around
But thought carefully,
And chose the colours he wanted to be.
He said: "I've made up my mind.
I want to be all the colours of the
rainbow."
But it was too late
Because the bumble bee
Had already become black striped
And yellow striped,
From the top of his head
To the tips of his toes.

I FEEL SICK

Teacher thinks I'm down in the dumps.
Grandpa winks, says "Cheer up, grumps!"

I get itches, twitches, lumps,
Rashes, fever, spots and bumps.

Doc says measles. Mum says mumps.
Gran says "Chicken-pox, you chumps!"

I feel poorly. My head thumps.

CHOOSING FOOD

What do you want to eat?
Would you like some meat?
Or maybe something sweet?

What do you want
What do you want
What do you want to eat?

We'll buy it
And fry it
And tuck in
And try it.

How do you feel
About that for a meal?

We'll make it
And bake it
And slice it
And take it.

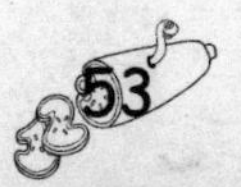

How do you feel
About that for a meal?

We'll baste it
And taste it
Cos we mustn't
Waste it.

So how do you feel
How do you feel
How do you feel
About that for a meal?

Well, what do you want to eat?
Would you like some meat?
Or maybe something sweet?

What do you want
What do you want
What do you want to eat?

SAD GRANDAD

Grandad John, Grandad John,
Your hair was black but now it's gone
As white as feathers on a swan,
But why are you so woebegone?
Just be happy, Grandad John.

Grandad John, Grandad John,
Your skin has gone like thin chiffon
Hung loosely on your skellington.
Now please don't look so put upon.
Do be happy, Grandad John.

Grandad John, Grandad John,
Your eyes are dull where they once shone.
Grandad John, Grandad John,
Your cake has eighty candles on.
Happy birthday, Grandad John!

A 1-2-3-4 RHYME

A one-two-three-four
Once upon a time rhyme.
A one-two-three-four
What a pantomime rhyme.

A one-two-three-four
Beanstalk Jack'll climb rhyme.
A one-two-three-four
Beans weren't worth a dime rhyme.

A one-two-three-four
Cinders, watch the time rhyme.
A one-two-three-four
Midnight's going to chime rhyme.

A one-two-three-four
What a pantomime rhyme.
A one-two-three-four
Every Christmas Time rhyme.

MOODY, MARDY, MOANY, MO

When you're sad,
How do you know?
Moody, mardy, moany, mo.

No one to play with.
Nowhere to go.
Moody, mardy, moany, mo.

Nothing to do
And nothing to show.
Moody, mardy, moany, mo.

Tick-a-time slowly,
Slowly slow.
Moody, mardy, moany, mo.

It's a cloud you sit below.
Moody, mardy, moany, mo.

WELLINGTON BOOT

A patch of earth
Called What-Is-It-Worth
Contained a seed
Called Big-As-A-Bead
Which grew a shoot
Called Wellington Boot
Which fed a snail
Called Tickle-My-Tail
Which fattened a bird
Called Whistle-A-Word
Which fed a cat
Called Acrobat
Which climbed a tree
Called Knuckle-And-Knee
Cut by an axe
Called Income Tax
That freed the seed
Called Big-As-A-Bead
That fell on the earth
Called What-Is-It-Worth
That grew the shoot
Called Wellington Boot

That fed the snail
Called Tickle-My-Tail
That fattened the bird
Called Whistle-A-Word
That fed the cat
Called Acrobat
That climbed the tree
Called Knuckle-And-Knee
Cut by the axe
Called Income Tax
That freed the seed
Called Big-As-A-Bead
And over and over
And over and over
And over and over again!

ACTING AS IF WE'RE DRAGONS

Let's imagine we're dragons. See who's best.
Pretend you're asleep inside your nest...
Then stretch as you emerge from reptile rest...
Yawn... and growl from deep inside your chest...
Press your stomach... dream of something to digest...

Shake yourself... and breathe out thick, black smoke...
Cough a bit... because it makes you choke.
Then rub your eyes... and move like you just woke...

Slowly stare out from your mountain lair...
Snarl... and try to make your nostrils
flare...
Now suck... to fill your fiery lungs with
air...

Let's see you exercise your lethal claws...
Expose those rows of teeth between
your jaws...
Then scratch your ancient scars from
dragon wars...

Stand up slowly... huge and hard as nails.
Flex those muscles underneath your
scales...
Now set your sights on distant hills and
vales...

And flap your arms as if they're heavy
wings...
Listen to the way the high wind sings...
As you fly towards the lands of kings.

Lick your lips... and keep your cruel eyes peeled...
Though you need to feed, your wounds have hardly healed
From your fight with a knight with sword and shield.

You're dizzy and weak before you arrive.
This time, you wonder if you will survive.
It's dangerous to hunt in the human hive.

But hunger hurts. It stabs your guts like five hundred knives.
See that food below you... ? Go into a dive...
Rip apart everything down there alive... !

WHAT'S SO SPECIAL ABOUT SIXTY-THREE?

When you and me and sixty-three
Called in a café for cups of tea,
You bought yours and paid for me
But sixty-three got his for free.

When you and me and sixty-three
Found that we just couldn't agree,
You gave me the third degree
But sixty-three just watched TV.

When you and me and sixty-three
Got caught in The Great Catastrophe,
We were rushed to casualty
But sixty-three just grazed his knee.

When you and me and sixty-three
Were sent to work in the factory,
We two were held in slavery
But sixty-three got paid a fee

When you and me and sixty-three
Were put in jail for burglary,
They hung us from the gallows tree
But sixty-three got given a key.

ONCE UPON A TIME

I once stayed up
Throughout the night
To count the stars in Heaven,
And by the time
That it was light
I'd reached eleventy-seven.

NUMBER, NUMBER, CUT A CUCUMBER

Close those
Eyes and
Start to
Slumber.
Moonlight
Cool as
A cu-
Cumber.

Dream you're
Dancing:
Tango,
Rumba
On a
Bridge a-
Cross the
Humber.

Watch the
River
While you
Slumber.
Water's
Wet. Those
Logs are
Lumber.

While they
Float by,
Count the
Number.
Night-night
Sleep tight
Snore and
Slumber.

DIFFERENT THINGS

What's the roof that's never wet?
Waterproof is never wet.
Tell me pets that need no vet?
Carpets won't require a vet.

Find me phones that never ring.
Saxaphones'll never ring.
And which choirs seldom sing?
Electric wires seldom sing.

Name some ants that aren't so small.
Elephants are big, not small.
Name a you that isn't you.
A female sheep is ewe, not you!

ARGUMENT

Yesterday, my best friend came
home with me. We played a game
of football, until I became
far too rough. I was to blame
when his ball burst. End of game.
He called me a naughty name.
I got cross, called him the same,
So he went home. Now that's a shame.

WHEN I'M OLD

Tell me , matey,
When I'm eighty,
Will I be bones?
Will I be skin?
Will I be thinnerty-thinnerty-thin?
Or, when I'm eighty, weighty, matey?

WHERE SID THE SPIDER HID

Sid the spider hid
Under the toilet lid.

He didn't! He did.
He didn't! He did.
I bet you a quid he did.
He didn't! He did.
He didn't! He did.
Under the toilet lid.
I kid you not, he did.

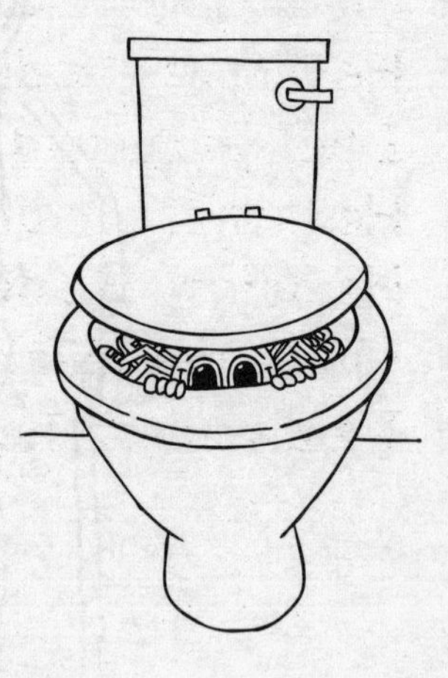

Sid the spider hid
This little arachnid
Who build his silky grid
Under the toilet lid.

He didn't! He did.
He didn't! He did.
I bet you a quid he did.

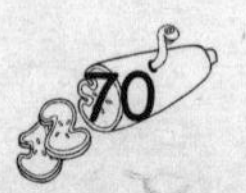

He didn't! He did.
He didn't! He did.
Under the toilet lid.
I kid you not, he did.

Sid the spider hid
But slipped one day and slid.
We heard his eight feet skid
And bid goodbye to Sid
Then flushed the loo, we did
And so got rid of Sid
Who swam off like a squid.

He didn't! He did.
He didn't! He did.
I bet you a quid he did.
He didn't! He did.
He didn't! He did.
Under the toilet lid.
I kid you not, he did.

WHAT DO I LOOK LIKE?

(written with children from
St Edmund's Nursery School, Bradford)

Do I look like an elephant or a horse?
No! I look like Magic Man, of course!

Do I look like a snail or potato head?
No! I look like Magic Man, I said!

Do I look like a dragon or a train?
No! I look like Magic Man again!

Do I look like a baby or a toy car?
No! I look like Magic Man. Ha! Ha!

Do I look like long hair with a red ribbon?
No! I look like Magic Man. Stop kiddin'!

Do I look like no one or play dough?
No! I look like Magic Man, you know!

Do I look like a mouse or a fishing net?
No! I look like Magic Man. Don't forget!

Do I look like a swing, a slide or a tree?
No! I look like Magic Man. That's me!

Do I look like a worm or a dog or a cat?
No! I look like Magic Man. That's that!

THE REPLACEMENT

When sixty-six
Clickety-clicks
Who shall we use instead?

Why, we'll do fine
With ninety-nine
Standing on his head.

WHEELS

There are wheels on bikes and trikes and cars.
So where are the wheels on chocolate bars?
And where are the wheels on old jam jars?
And where are the wheels on shooting stars?

There are wheels on trolleys and lorries and vans.
So where are the wheels on frying pans?
And where are the wheels on bottles and cans?
And where are the wheels on football fans?

There are wheels on trains and planes and beds (except flower beds).
So where are the wheels on sleepyheads?
And where are the wheels on garden sheds?
And where are the wheels on dolls and teds?

Wheels through puddles all say *SWISHHHHHHHHHHHHHHHHH!*
But where are the wheels on a frozen fish?
And where are the wheels on a Turkish dish?
And where are the wheels on a sticka-licka-rish?

Wheels in watches make them go.
But where are the wheels on a cuppa cocoa?
And where are the wheels on *Yo! Ho! Ho!*
And where are the wheels on eeny... meeny... miney... mo?

There are wheels on lots of children's toys.
But where are the wheels on saveloys?
And where are the wheels on *"STOP THAT NOISE!"*?
And where are the wheels on girls and boys?

PACKED LUNCHES

While the school dinner-queue
Pushes and punches,
All of us pupils
With packed lunches
Sit around the playground
In small bunches.

Over each lunch-box
One of us hunches,
And, while the dinner-queue
Pushes and punches,
We chew cheese butties with
Munch-munch-munches,

Eat our apples with
Scrunch-scrunch-scrunches,
Gobble our crisps with
Crunch-crunch-crunches.
Meanwhile, the dinner-queue
Pushes and punches.

We're all glad we
Bring packed lunches.

SOME SALAMANDERS

Some salamanders say your name.
Some salamanders pray for fame.
Some salamanders slay and maim.

Some salamanders may show shame.
Some salamanders, they take aim.
Some salamanders sway when lame.

Some salamanders lay the blame.
Some salamanders pay that claim.
Some salamanders weigh the same.

Some salamanders play the game.
Some salamanders stay quite tame.
Some salamanders wade through flame.

AT SEVENTY-ONE O'CLOCK

At five to seventy-one o'clock
The king just licked a stick of rock
And hid behind a hollyhock
And claimed that he was taking stock.
His feet were bare. He wore a frock
And, on his head, a purple sock.
The queen sneaked off to phone a doc
But all the lines were chock-a-block.

While, with a tickly tack-teck-tock,
Our pocket watches ran amok
And time became a laughing-stock
For chiming seventy-one o'clock.

The ticks on Bo Peep's sheep went tock,
Stampeding her entire flock.
The cuckoo in the cuckoo clock
Shot about like a shuttlecock.
Old Sherlock Holmes just shook with shock.
"Illogical!" said Mr Spock.
And poor Professor Havelock
Just muttered "Utter poppycock!"

While, with a tickly tack-teck-tock,
Our pocket watches ran amok
And time became a laughing-stock
For chiming seventy-one o'clock
seventy-one o'clock.

CAN WE SIT APART, MISS?

Please, miss! Christine broke my heart,
miss.
Tipped her water on my art, miss.

Made me cry, miss, which is why, miss,
Like my painting, I'm not dry, miss.

So next time, miss, for a start, miss,
Please, please, can we sit apart, miss?

KICK A BALL

Kick a ball, kick a ball,
Kick a ball in Montreal.
Kick a ball, kick a ball,
Kick a ball in Cornwall.
Kick a ball, kick a ball,
Kick a ball in Bengal.
Kick a ball, kick a ball.

Kick it when I come to call.
Kick it up against a wall.
Kick it big or kick it small.
Kick it over there to Paul.
Kick it in a free-for-all.
Kick it if you've got the gall.

**Kick a ball, kick a ball,
Kick a ball in Montreal.
Kick a ball, kick a ball,
Kick a ball in Cornwall.
Kick a ball, kick a ball,
Kick a ball in Bengal.
Kick a ball, kick a ball.**

Kick it over something tall.
Kick it down a waterfall.
Kick it round the county hall.
Kick it in a shopping mall.
Kick it fast or at a crawl.
Kick it with a caterwaul.

Kick a ball, kick a ball,
Kick a ball in Montreal.
Kick a ball, kick a ball,
Kick a ball in Cornwall.
Kick a ball, kick a ball,
Kick a ball in Bengal.
Kick a ball, kick a ball.

BEWARE OF THE DOG

Bang on the door
Bang on the door
Bang on the door of sixty-four
But don't ignore their Labrador
Who'll give your leg a nasty gnaw
And leave it bleeding, red and raw
And terribly, terribly, terribly sore
And that's because a Labrador
Is naturally a carnivore.

Bang on the door
Bang on the door
Bang on the door of sixty-four
So long as you're sure you know the score
And not before, no, not before
You're well aware of what's in store.
Look at the jaw. Look at the paw.
Size of the tooth, size of the claw
And that's because a Labrador
Is naturally a carnivore.

Bang on the door
Bang on the door
Bang on the door of sixty-four...
If you dare!

TOSSING PANCAKES

"Alright!" says dad. "This should be fun.
Now let me show you how it's done.
Just watch what I do, everyone..."

Now, why've I got this dreadful feeling
Somehow soon we'll all be peeling
Pancakes off the kitchen ceiling?

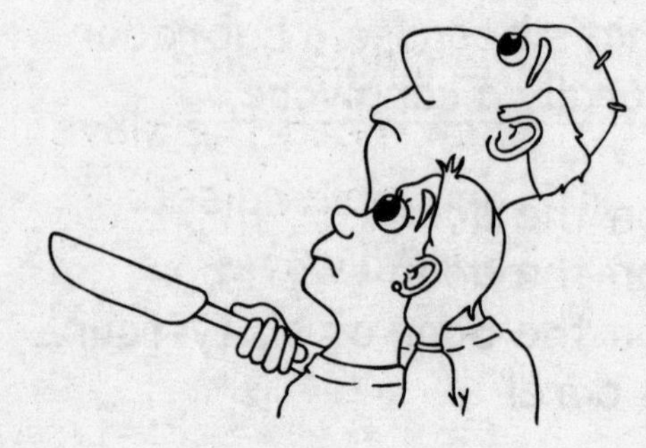

WISH

When you grow up
I hope you'll be
The seed that grew
Into a tree,

The breeze that blew
Into a storm,
The bee that caused
The hive to swarm,

The worm that turned
Into a snake,
The drip-drip-drip
That made a lake,

The single voice
That freed the slave,
The ripple raised
To tidal wave,

The beauty none
Have seen before,
The word which put
An end to war...

When you grow up
I hope you'll be
Better in every way
Than me.

Other Children's Books By Nick Toczek

Me And My Poems (Caboodle '08)

Read Me Out Loud! (Macmillan '07)

Dragons! The Musical (Golden Apple '05)

Dragons! (Macmillan '05)

The Dog Ate My Bus Pass (Macmillan '04)

Sleeping Beauty's Dream (Golden Apple '03)

Kick It! (Macmillan '02)

Number Parade (LDA '02)

Can Anyone Be As Gloomy As Me? (Hodder '00, republished '05)

Toothpaste Trouble (Macmillan '02)

The Dragon Who Ate Our School (Macmillan '00)

Never Stare at a Grizzly Bear (Macmillan '00)

Join In... Or Else! (Macmillan '00)

Dragons Everywhere (Macmillan '97)

Dragons (Macmillan '95)

Cats'n'Bats'n'Slugs'n'Bugs (Caboodle '08)